40 Days of Discipleship
Series 1

James Hermann Klaas

Foreword Ross Rains

ENDORSMENTS

What better pursuit in this life is there than to grow in one's relationship with the Lord through His Word and by His Spirit. 40 Days of Discipleship is a tool developed to help people deepen their participation with God and His Kingdom. I recommend that you try this resource and pass it along to others. - **Denys Blackmore, President/CEO, Every Home for Christ International - Canada**

If Jesus walked our earth today, how would he know his disciples? In his 40 days, Jim Klaas has captured the essence of building the disciplines that move us from Jesus talk to an empowered Jesus walk. - **Dr. Jonathan Lewis, Founder/President Go Global Network**

Anyone who wants to walk with God and be used by Him, must put down some discipleship roots. With 40 Days of Discipleship, timeless scriptural discipleship principles have been merged with a modern webcasting vehicle. Invest 5 minutes a day reflecting on the discipleship principle to experience transformation. - **Ragnar Oborn, Intercultural Communications Specialist**

In this series you will be drawn to feed on the Scriptures, to take definite steps of faith and will learn to network together through this simple, practical resource. - **Ross Rains, Founder of Pathfinders Ministry**

I think God is bigger, more powerful and more mysterious than I did before the 40 Days. - **H.Y.** (a young believer)

FOREWORD

This series, which Jim has crafted, addresses a serious gap in short-term missions' effectiveness. Typically, these outreaches of two or three weeks are motivated by the desire to serve far-away people groups with a specific set of needs. However, the true benefactors are those who go to serve, and it is your development as an influencer which really determines your lasting spiritual return for your project. In this series, you will be drawn to feed on the Scriptures, to take definite steps of faith and will learn to network together and work through this simple, practical resource.

The DNA of Discipleship (Series 1) provides a pre-trip developmental focus to elevate your spiritual health (no matter what your age and spiritual experience). Then upon returning, the next series, **The 5 Verbs of Learning** (Series 2), provides an after-trip focus on how to convert what you learning into action. Imagine! A start-to-finish, three month touch on your life as you launch this faith adventure. And consider one further benefit. Whether you are going to an area that speaks English, Spanish or French, you can connect and invite new friends to grow spiritually together with you, first by following your example, then by your active encouragement at a distance and followed by partnering together by passing this resource on to others both 'here and there' as others' begin their journey' with Jesus. You will truly 'inherit the nations' through this investment (Psalm 2:8).

I have known Jim for over 40 years with our own journeys intertwined in international service. He and his family served as field missionaries for 15 years in Latin America and Jim has invested in a dozen 2 week trips from North America.

I would recommend not sending another short-termer without the implementation of this resource if making disciples of Jesus is at the core of your service and if you want your contribution to have a lasting impact.

Ross Rains,

Founder of Pathfinders Ministry

London, Ontario, Canada

ACKNOWLEDGMENTS

This book reflects a journey of over 40 years in what has helped me grow as a learner of Jesus Christ. I wish I could list all who has helped me grow, the named and the unnamed, from those who first talked to me about Jesus Christ, to those leading Bible studies and home groups, to countless sermons, books, conferences and seminars on various continents and in different languages. It took more than a village to raise me! It seemed like God provided a whole army of people all over the world, whose good example I could imitate, whose patience to walk with me gave me comfort and whose grace allowed me to grow towards becoming all that the Lord intended.

The Lord did challenge me to 'ask big' on this project. I had been praying for an inheritance of the nations (Psalm 2:8) and I felt the Lord asking me "So how many do you want?"

My first thought was "a million" simply because it seemed like an uncountable number, like the stars in the sky. My next thought was that this seemed presumptuous and that "who was I to ask such a thing?" But I decided that the Lord is quite capable to do what He promises and that we probably err more in NOT asking enough than asking for too much (James 4:2). So my request stands. "Help me mobilize an uncountable number of labourers to help a countless number of people enjoy the blessing of knowing and serving God through Jesus Christ."

I hope that is your prayer as well. The promises of God are infinitely scalable and will never run out. Ask Him for an inheritance of the nations as you serve Him. Make disciples and help mobilize them everywhere.

I want to thank you for your investment in purchasing this book. Proceeds from this sale will help those in the Majority World participate in this series. They will have an opportunity to thank you someday.

I am indebted to Neil Cole (www.cmaresources.org) for his ideas on the DNA of Discipleship that have guided us in this series.

J H Klaas

The DNA of Discipleship

INTRODUCTION

In this series you will focus on HOW to grow as a learner of Jesus. It is not meant to provide information but action. Each participant should have access to their own copy and daily dedicate a few minutes to review the content and practice the activities. Each person can decide how best to learn from the material. The important thing is for you to *learn how to learn* from God. You are in charge of your personal learning. Observe yourself as you learn. What works? Where do you have difficulty?

It is recommended that once a week you get together with other participants and discuss what you have read and what you are learning. Come prepared to share what you think would be helpful: personal observations, questions and insights. This is a skill that also grows with practice. You may find some of the questions for reflection or activity questions helpful to guide your sharing.

Be prepared to jot down ideas and questions and for God to interrupt you at different times with insights or growth opportunities that will form part of your learning. Sermons, other reading and life events all form part of God's curriculum in your apprenticeship.

Ask God to work supernaturally in and through you. Invite others to join you. If they are not physically near you, invite them to do this online. (Sign up at www.networkchurch.ca) and they will receive a lesson per day via email. You can then meet via a phone call or via a computer conference. The lessons can be viewed on a smart phone.

This series will help form the genetic code in your learning from Jesus as His disciple and will form the pattern that others may imitate from your life. This is an exciting opportunity to grow oneself and to help others in their learning journey.

We recommend that you use this series for preparation in going on a mission's trip, then share it where you go (other language versions are available) then do the next series when you come back.

If you are receiving people who recommend this series, consider yourselves as missionaries as you pass this on to others. We all share in the global challenge.

Day 1: How did Jesus make disciples?

1 John 1:1-2

That which was from the beginning, which we have heard, which we have seen with our eyes, which we have looked at and our hands have touched—this we proclaim concerning the Word of life. The life appeared; we have seen it and testify to it, and we proclaim to you the eternal life, which was with the Father and has appeared to us.

How did Jesus make disciples? You can spend a lifetime on this question. Let's observe what is recorded in the Scriptures. Jesus spent time with his disciples. They ate, talked, walked and shared life together for 3 years. Jesus asked them questions, gave them impossible tasks, deliberately broke traditions and challenged their thinking. He angered religious leaders and welcomed outcasts. He healed on the Sabbath and asked them to feed 5000 people. He had them watch miracles at weddings and on death beds. Sometimes He let them fail and he would help them learn. Sometimes He let them succeed but told them not put confidence in their successes. He demonstrated that he had absolute authority over the weather and demons and life itself. It was not about 'God theory'. It was a constant interaction with God, scary, unsettling and life transforming. Welcome to 40 days of discipleship: one minute per day.

For Reflection:

- What would you like to learn in the next 40 days?

- Compare your experience with Jesus and the Scripture passage above.

Make Life Count:

- Write a short prayer expressing what you would like Jesus to do in your life through this time.

The Jesus Model

Day 2: Why 40 Days?

Matthew 4:1-2

Then Jesus was led by the Spirit into the wilderness to be tempted by the devil. After fasting forty days and forty nights, he was hungry.

We have chosen 40 days for this activity since the number 40 in the Bible represents a time of testing out of which something significant happens. There were 40 days of rain at the time of Noah. Moses was 40 days with God when he received the 10 commandments. The people of Israel were 40 years in the desert. Jesus was tempted by Satan for 40 days. A pregnancy is 40 weeks long out of which a new life is born. 40 days, almost 6 weeks, is the length of Lent, traditionally used for reflection and preparation for Easter. It will be long enough to stretch you but short enough that you can focus on this without feeling you are promising to do something you can't complete. Pray and ask Jesus for an ever deeper desire to learn from Him over these 40 days. And don't worry about 'getting it all' on the first try. We offer a second series that reviews what we cover here with additional challenges.

For Reflection:

- What is the biggest obstacle you face that affects your learning about God?

Make Life Count:

- Spend a minute thanking God for everything that has happened to bring you to where you are today.

The Jesus Model

Day 3: Choose your lifestyle?

Matthew 28:19-20

Therefore go and make disciples of all nations, baptizing them in the name of the Father and of the Son and of the Holy Spirit, and teaching them to obey everything I have commanded you. And surely I am with you always, to the very end of the age.

Jesus said, "Go and make disciples". Not as an optional suggestion but as the main way that his kingdom would grow and bless the world. It wasn't an advanced option for the truly committed but the normal pattern for normal people to grow.

Being Jesus' disciple involves knowing something, being something and doing something. We follow his example and learn his methods. It is personal but it is not individualistic. It is not a course but a lifestyle. It is not just information but it is applied in experience.

In the simplest form, ***disciples are learners who journey together to follow a teacher in a relational process, then repeat the same pattern with others.*** Jesus is both the teacher and subject matter. We learn from Him and about Him. God uses the Scriptures, other people and life's circumstances to help us learn to change and become more like Him. It is knowing, being and doing with Jesus as our teacher.

For Reflection:

- What type of teacher has Jesus been for you?

- How does this Scripture passage make you feel?

Make Life Count:

- Write down one question you would like to ask Jesus about how he has been "with you always" over the years. Then talk to him about that.

The Jesus Model

Day 4: Embrace the "be with" strategy

Mark 3:14

He appointed twelve that they might be with him and that he might send them out to preach.

Acts 4:13

When they saw the courage of Peter and John and realized that they were unschooled, ordinary men, they were astonished and they took note that these men had been with Jesus.

Discipleship in the Gospels was a relational process where Jesus chose 12 to be 'with him'. After he left the earth, even those who opposed Christ recognized the disciples as having been with Jesus .They sounded like him, they taught like him and they worked like him. They learned to do what he did. The 'Being with' strategy meant guiding and accompanying others in real life.

Do you know another Jesus' follower with whom you can read the Bible and discuss what you are learning? Something special happens when 2 or 3 people gather in Jesus' name. Invite a friend to join you and meet for a coffee to share ideas and questions about what you are discovering. Discuss verses you have highlighted or comments you have written. Discipleship learning could start in a 15 minute coffee break. God is an amazing connector of people. Ask for his help to connect with someone to join together in this learning journey.

For Reflection:

- Who has helped you so far in your learning journey with God? How have they been 'with you'?
- Who could you connect with to make this more meaningful?

Make Life Count:

- If someone has helped you in your spiritual journey, write her/him a short email and say 'Thank you".

The Jesus Model

Day 5: Like learning to ride a bike

1 John 3:18

Dear children, let us not love with words or speech but with actions and in truth.

Discipleship is like learning to ride a bike. You need to know how the breaks, pedals and handlebars work. You need to be in balance and you need to do the pedaling and steering. But how did you actually learn to ride a bike? Often someone runs alongside and holds the bike, coaches what to do next and then gradually lets go. Sometimes we put on training wheels as a temporary help to keep our balance. The bike does not work quite as well but it gives a feeling of the experience until we are confident enough to take the extra wheels off.

These 40 days are like spiritual training wheels or having someone run alongside you. These exercises will help but they are just training wheels. As you gain confidence you will discover your best patterns to more freely learn from God. And like bike riding, you will feel the wind on your face, explore creation and discover a deeper walk with the Lord.

For Reflection:

- How did you learn to ride a bike?

- How does that experience compare to learning to learn from Jesus?

Make Life Count:

- Decide one thing you can do to love someone through an action or deed today then do it.

The Jesus Model

Day 6: Develop healthy habits

Luke 2:52

And Jesus grew in wisdom and stature, and in favor with God and man.

Don't underestimate the value of small healthy habits practiced over a long period of time. This is true in how we eat, exercise or grow as learners of Jesus. Scripture reading, even something as brief as a few minutes with God, will accumulate benefit over time. A daily prayer for laborers takes seconds but keep your eyes open for God to work. Inviting and encourage another to share a weekly encounter to discuss what you are learning together using the questions for nurturing relationships can have an enormous impact in laying a spiritual foundation and can be a most valuable investment of time. Of course without Jesus in the center of these activities, they can seem like hoop-jumping but with Jesus in the center, these habits can significantly deepen us as His followers.

For Reflection:

- How did Jesus grow in the areas mentioned in Luke 2:52?
- How do you keep habits from becoming religious duty?

Make Life Count:

- Thank God for one habit that helps you in life.

The Jesus Model

Day 7: Look for patterns

John 10:40

Then Jesus went back across the Jordan to the place where John had been baptizing in the early days. There he stayed.

If you want to learn, look for patterns. A big part of our learning is finding and imitating patterns of the ways to think, be and do. Most of what we learn is caught and not taught. Have you ever noticed how children can walk, talk and laugh like their parents? They were never given lessons to do that. It is quite helpful to observe patterns in Jesus' life and use these to guide our responses to circumstances: what to think, what to say and what to do. What did Jesus do when he was tired or discouraged? How did he respond to the needy and to the self-satisfied? How did he talk with his disciples and with the religious leaders? How did he use stories and questions? How did he use the Scriptures and prayer? These all provide patterns which we can learn from and imitate in our discipleship.

For Reflection:

• What patterns in Jesus' life have you observed? (Why did he return to the place where he was baptized?)

• What patterns did you learn from your parents?

Make Life Count:

• List one pattern from your family when growing up that you really like and one you really dislike. Decide to make patterns you like.

The Jesus Model

Meet this week to discuss JESUS IS OUR MODEL: Days 1 to 7

Jesus is our model in everything. We need to return to him again and again to see what he taught and how he put it into practice. While we can't imitate him in everything (he mostly walked, rarely rode a donkey and didn't travel more than 100 km from home), we can ask ourselves how we can practice "to be with" (Day 4) as a relational strategy for making disciples. Discipleship is not a course, a study material or a training programme. Discipleship is a living relationship of walking together, sharing deeply and meaningfully in knowing and serving God together.

In order to make disciples, people need *a vision of what to do, a method to show them how* and *the confidence that they are able.* All this is undergirded by the power of the Holy Spirit. We want to help provide these three elements for the Spirit to work.

Why did we choose this format of 40 days if it is purely relational? We know this material is incomplete, but it is a start. Our hope is that a daily reminder arriving either by cell phone, laptop or via a printed book, will build a rhythm of a daily habit of seeking God and learning. Weekly get-togethers are to discuss highlights, to help integrate the Scriptures into the unique needs of every participant and to help us stay rooted in our relationship with him.

All of this is simple enough that anyone can imitate it and pass it on. The fact that you opened this link indicates that you are a learner wanting to help other learners. You are a key contributor in the process of multiplication. Throughout this course we would like to provide more resources. In fact every 7 days, along with the regular 40 Days material you will be provided a link to these resources.

Your preparation:
1. What do you observe in Jesus' life that you desire in your own?
2. Look for patterns of what He is doing in or around you. It could be repeated thoughts, or ideas that are reinforced through different circumstances.
3. As a leader, are you practicing healthy learning habits? What type of example are you to others who are just starting out?

4.   Imagine yourself running alongside the others in the group as they learn to ride a bike. Don't hang on too tightly. The idea is to help them get their balance and develop skill so they can ride on their own.

The meeting:

Keep it short and conversational. Some suggested questions:

How has the experience of the first week been? What has been difficult or easy? What do you think God is saying and how have you responded? How can we help each other?

Day 8: Quench your thirst

John 7:37-38

On the last and greatest day of the festival, Jesus stood and said in a loud voice, "Let anyone who is thirsty come to me and drink. Whoever believes in me, as Scripture has said, rivers of living water will flow from within them."

Discipleship is a learning marathon. It is life-long and it is life-changing. It is remarkable that God uses something as simple as reading and responding to the Scriptures to make it happen. What are you reading today that is inviting you to action?

God's promises are like that. They often come with a promised blessing and a condition. Something you need to do, or ask, or count or believe. Sometimes the condition is clear, like in this example 'Whoever is thirsty come to me and drink and from his inner most being will flow rivers of living water". You have to be thirsty? You have to come to Jesus and you have to drink THEN there is some kind of spiritual overflow that happens: the Spirit bubbles up and flows out of you like a river. Have you ever felt that happen?

For Reflection:

- What is the thirstiest you have ever been?
- How has your relationship with Jesus been like water to the thirsty?

Make Life Count:

- Take a bottle of water on a walk and at some point stop and take a drink. Pay close attention to the sensations you experience. Ask God to bubble through you with His living water.

The DNA of Discipleship

Divine Truth

Day 9: Become like a newborn babe

2 Peter 2:2,3

Like newborn babies, crave pure spiritual milk, so that by it you may grow up in your salvation, now that you have tasted that the Lord is good..

People need food to grow. A baby needs pure milk. 1 Peter 2:2 says "like new born babes, long for the pure milk of the word that you may grow thereby". Interacting with the Scriptures provides spiritual milk which helps us grow.

Milk that comes from a nursing mother is pure milk. It is clean and not diluted with anything. It is easy to digest. It has the mother's antibodies that help fight infection. It is not made with dirty water. How does this relate to discipleship? We need to read the simpler parts of the Scriptures first, like the Gospels that talk about Jesus. A new born eats many times a day in small amounts that are easier to digest. These will be milk for you to help you grow, especially if you can reflect on these verses and respond in some way. It may take some time but you will see a difference.

For Reflection:

- What part of the Scriptures reminds you of milk?
- When have you been most thirsty for this milk?

Make Life Count:

- At some point today, take a break and drink a cold glass of milk. While you do that, think about how God has nurtured you over the years. Thank Him.

Divine Truth

Day 10: Get off the bottle!

1 Corinthians 3:2

He told them, "The harvest is plentiful, but the workers are few.
Ask the Lord of the harvest, therefore, to send out workers into
his harvest field.

If bottle feeding went on permanently throughout a person's life, it would be very odd. Imagine a group of 60 year olds drinking milk from baby bottles? Normally babies, around 6 months of age, learn to eat solid foods little by little. They start with soft stuff. It is messy. They squish it with their fingers and rub it on their hair. Food gets all over the place. But they eventually learn to feed themselves.
We need to do the same in discipleship. You may start with the short verses, which is all you need. Later you will want to read the whole chapter where it is from or to understand what that book of the Bible says. At some point you will want to read through the whole Bible. This is a natural part of the growing process. You can select the passage reference and access the whole chapter to read the verse in context. Try it when you feel a need for more and experiment with what works the best.

For Reflection:

- Do you think you should be eating solid food from the Scriptures? (It is perfectly fine to realize you are not ready for that yet.)
- How have you experienced feeding yourself in the Scriptures?

Make Life Count:

- Ask God for His plan to learn the Scriptures considering where you are right now.

The DNA of Discipleship

Divine Truth

Day 11: Spend seven minutes with God

Psalm 1:3

That person is like a tree planted by streams of water,
which yields its fruit in season
and whose leaf does not wither—
whatever they do prospers.

One way to engage the Scriptures is a pattern called **7 minutes with God.** You do 5 things which you can number on the fingers of one hand.

1.   Pray and ask God to open your heart to learn from the Scriptures. We ask the Holy Spirit to teach us.

2.   Read the passage from a Bible. If we are just starting out, it should be something that is good for beginners.

3.   Read it again slowly, savoring the ideas. Chew on them. Think about any questions provided with the reading.

4.   Pick a thought or phrase that stands out which you can focus on throughout the day. To help remember, record ideas in the comment section for that verse or bookmark the verse as a favorite. Think especially how you can respond in some way.

5.   Pray and ask God to use it in your life.

These are like training wheels to help you meet with God as you read the Scriptures. Later you can be much less structured and try different patterns.

For Reflection:

- How important is it to daily commune with God.
- What is the best time of day to make it happen?

Make Life Count:

- Start the Seven Minutes with God in one of the Gospels of Matthew, Mark, Luke or John. (Feel free to read elsewhere, but this is a good starting point if you are looking for a suggestion.)

Divine Truth

Day 12: Read God-breathed Scriptures

2 Timothy 3:16-17

All Scripture is God-breathed and is useful for teaching, rebuking, correcting and training in righteousness, so that the servant of God may be thoroughly equipped for every good work.

How do the Scriptures work in our lives? The Apostle Paul said to Timothy that *"all Scripture is God-breathed and is useful for teaching, rebuking, correcting and training in righteousness."*
God breathes the Scriptures out through the writers and we breathe them in when we read them. When that happens we get to know the path of Jesus, when we get off it, how to get back on and to enjoy the result of seeing our lives change.
There are different ways we receive the Scriptures through: hearing, reading, studying, memorizing and meditating. We need all 5, especially how to meditate on the Scriptures. Like a cow which eats grass, then chews over it very slowly, we chew over the Scriptures and think about them continually. This nourishes our soul and shows us how to think, and be and do. Our daily plan reminds us to go back to the Scriptures and we can try different times of day to read the Scripture portions.

For Reflection:

- What does it mean that the Scriptures are God-breathed?

- How do they keep us on the path of Jesus?

Make Life Count:

- Practice meditating on today's verse by repeatedly reading it out loud and each time emphasize a different word: / **ALL** Scripture is God-breathed and …/ All **SCRIPTURE** is God-breathed…/ All Scripture **IS** God-breathed…/etc.

Divine Truth

Day 13: Look for the unexpected

2 Corinthians 5:17

Therefore, if anyone is in Christ, the new creation has come: The old has gone, the new is here!

Look around for something unexpected: a new opportunity, a new desire, a new ability, a new connection, a new possibility, a new understanding or a new relationship. The old is gone! He is making all things new. What does that look like? What new patterns do you see? What are you doing with these patterns?

Something may still look the same, but perhaps you can understand it in a new way? Life is difficult and sometimes downright painful. Where is God doing something new inside of the old? How can you pray differently? Are thoughts from your Scripture reading, giving you new understanding in these situations? What might be invisible to the human eye, that you suspect that God is doing? How do we find out about that? Who can you discuss this with?

For Reflection:

- In what way does God make things new?
- Why might it be difficult to recognize the new?

Make Life Count:

- Open the Bible and look at the index. Check off the books you have read or circle a few that you would like to read. Keep this in mind when you need to choose the next book of the Bible you will read.

Divine Truth

Day 14: Say 'Yes and amen'

2 Corinthians 1:20

Keep your eyes open for promises in the Bible where God commits himself to do something. This should immediately get our attention. We are joint heirs with Christ which means that many things that belong to Jesus can be for us as well. The promises of God will never run out, which means if one person claims them or a million people claim them, then they are still fully available. We always have enough and God will not be limited because of excessive demands for his blessings.

When you see a promise where the condition is met in Christ, then write the date into the margin and pray and ask God to give what he is promising. The promises tend to operate around a deeper relationship with God, a greater influence in helping other and in leaving a spiritual legacy that affects the nations. Keep your eyes open for these. It may take time to see the results but they are all 'Yes' and 'Amen' in Jesus.

For Reflection:

- What promises in the Bible are important to you?
- Which ones do you not understand?

Make Life Count:

- Find one promise in the Bible and write in today's date and pray: "Jesus is Yes and Amen for this promise". (If you want a place to start, go to yesterday's verse: John 7:37-38.)

The DNA of Discipleship

Divine Truth

Meet this week to discuss DIVINE TRUTH : Days 8 to 14

These two weeks of the 40 Days of Discipleship focuses on *Divine truth* through reading the Bible.

How does a mother feed her baby? From newborn up to 6 months of age, exclusive breastfeeding is recommended. At first the baby drinks the equivalent of 5 ml, a tablespoon, of milk. By one week of age the stomach doubles in size. She will feed every two hours day and night: a little at a time and very often.

At about 6 months of age solid is food is introduced in the form of a soft porridge. Later fruits and vegetables are given all mashed up, and only later is food offered in small pieces. Eventually the child learns to feed herself but not without making a considerable mess on the floor, their clothing, the table and anyone who is within arm's reach.

Remember the person who is new to the Bible is just starting to learn. Help them to find one helpful thought from this week's lessons and don't over load them with 10 great ideas. They have a lifetime ahead to learn the intricacies. First let them taste and see that the Lord is good.

The daily devotional time, 7 Minutes with God, is a basic building block in discipleship. Remember the structure is like training wheels on a 2 wheeler bike. The short term goal is to be able to expand the devotional methods once the basic process is learned. But it serves as a good starting point. This is a tool worth memorizing so it is easily shared.

1. Be sure you practiced a daily meeting with God yourself. If you have done Series 1 before then you should quickly review the content. If it is your first time through then be sure to give it your best attention for your own growth.
2. Ask an open question to encourage sharing like "What stood out to you from the last 7 days?" And be prepared to share a simple

thought of what you found helpful or challenging. (Your sharing should not be longer that what others say.)

3. Enjoy the time together. Listen and rejoice in small victories.

4. Keep the meeting brief enough that the person will want to do it again. It is good when the meeting ends and the person 'wants more' as they will come again next week.

Day 15: Feast on the Scriptures

Jeremiah 15:16

When your words came, I ate them;
they were my joy and my heart's delight,
for I bear your name,
Lord God Almighty.

You don't have to understand nutrition in order to eat. And you certainly can starve if you understand nutrition but don't eat. This is true with spiritual growth as well. We don't always understand the Scriptures although they can still make a difference to help us grow. Or the opposite is that we can understand the Scriptures but be starving because we are not 'eating' the bread of life regularly.
I find it helpful when I read a passage, to focus on what is clear. I might see where I need to grow, or where I can grip onto an encouraging truth about God. I might see a good example to imitate or a bad one to avoid. I might find a promise to claim or a specific command to obey. My imagination might be stirred about what God could do by seeing how he has acted in the past. Let your Scripture reading be food that keeps you growing.

For Reflection:

- Can you think of an example of something you don't understand but still is encouraging?

- What can you do with what you do not understand?

Make Life Count:

- In your 7 minutes with God, imagine you are eating the Scriptures and not just reading them. What is the difference?

Divine Truth

Day 16: Learn to eat every day

John10:10
The thief comes only to steal and kill and destroy; I have come that they may have life, and have it to the full.

You don't have to eat delicious food all the time for it to nourish you. Sometimes Scripture reading can be dry. This does not mean it is not nourishing. We feel we should have some deep insights from the Scriptures to share or we should have experienced some dramatic manifestations of God's presence. We get disappointed when that doesn't always happen.

Sometimes normal life is quietly growing without a great fanfare. It is putting one foot ahead of the other on a long journey. It is saying 'no' to something harmful. Or it is showing up instead of giving up. It is OK if we have no dramatic insights or stories to tell but we have become nurtured from continuing in the Scriptures. We have sought to be faithfully present. This too is miraculous.

For Reflection:

- When do the Scriptures seem most delicious to you?
- How does Jesus give 'life to the full'?

Make Life Count:

- Write down one thing you want stopped that 'steal, kills or destroys' in your life/ family/relationships/ job. Ask Jesus to bring His full life into what you have listed.

Divine Truth

Day 17: Do something to learn

James 1:22

Do not merely listen to the word, and so deceive yourselves. Do what it says.

Practice doing something with what you learn. Experience helps cement the truth and gives great satisfaction to the learning. This seems obvious but the more we can actively use what we are learning, the more encouraging and real it will become. We are to be doers of the Word and not just hearers. We don't earn favor by putting truth into practice but we gain the benefit of seeing the truth function according to its intended purposes. While our experience may be incomplete practice steps, it serves to get us moving in the right direction. If we combine this practice with reflection, bringing the experience back to the Scriptures, it is truly transformative. Learning becomes a journey that is purposeful and satisfying.

For Reflection:

- What are you doing with what you are learning each day?
- What new experiences do you think God has prepared for you?

Make Life Count:

- Use the form below to tell us what action steps you have found most helpful or suggestions that could be helpful for others who do this series.

Divine Truth

Day 18: See Christ as the Center

Hosea 6:3

Let us acknowledge the Lord;
let us press on to acknowledge him.
As surely as the sun rises,
he will appear;
he will come to us like the winter rains,
like the spring rains that water the earth.

Jesus Christ is to be the center of our attention. He is to be the "hub of the wheel" of our lives and we cannot expect to go far in our Christian life without the power and stability that the hub provides. As the Apostle Paul reminds us, "it is no longer we who live but Christ who lives in us, and the new life we live, we live by faith in the Son of God who loves us and gave Himself for us."
And so we need to be careful that the activities in our discipleship do not replace Jesus as of prime importance. We need constant reminding to keep our focus on Jesus and not just the training wheels as we practice.

For Reflection:

- When have some habits distracted your attention from Jesus?
- When have they helped?

Make Life Count:

- List a few helpful or harmful habits you would like to change.

Divine Truth

Day 19: Develop a restful relationship

Matthew 11:28-30

"Come to me, all you who are weary and burdened, and I will give you rest. Take my yoke upon you and learn from me, for I am gentle and humble in heart, and you will find rest for your souls. For my yoke is easy and my burden is light."

What would Jesus say about your learning so far? Imagine him sitting across the room and he invites you to tell him about your journey. He asks you if you are tired. He promises rest. He says he is gentle and humble of heart. He understands your weaknesses and struggles. How would you respond in terms of integrity, transparency and vulnerability? Where can you invite him be part of an area of your life that perhaps you felt was out of bounds or that he didn't care about? He called this relationship a 'yoke', like two oxen pulling together. He said it was well-fitting that made difficult things easier to carry. With a yoke, two animals can pull more than twice of what each can do alone. It is like riding a tandem bicycle and suggests journeying together; the idea of being very much accompanied and being a co-participant in the revealed plans of God.

For Reflection:

- Who can you discuss your ideas with about these questions?
- Why did Jesus call his invitation a 'yoke'?

Make Life Count:

- Try taking a break in the day where you deliberately rest in Jesus. For 5 minutes, imagine him helping you carry burdens that are heavy for you.

Divine Truth

Day 20: Abide in Jesus the vine

John 15:5

I am the vine; you are the branches. If you remain in me and I in you, you will bear much fruit; apart from me you can do nothing.

We have discussed the DNA of discipleship,but without Jesus these things are just religious activity. Think about Jesus being our life. Think about how he saves and frees us from the devil's work. How he works in us, guides us, teaches us, and prays for us. He calls us friends. We are to abide in Him and let Him live his life through us. We are to obey what he taught us and let him be the rock on which we build our lives. We are to imitate him even to the point of taking up the cross, identifying with his death and living the new life he provides. We need to be sure to build our learning around Jesus and not have discipleship activities be an end in themselves. This is a challenge in spiritual formation: to keep Christ central.

For Reflection:

- What causes you to lose your focus on Jesus?
- What causes you to try to do things "apart from" Jesus?

Make Life Count:

- Sit quietly and imagine with each breath you take, Jesus' life is flowing through you and with each exhalation your worries and sins are being cast on Him.

Divine Truth

Day 21: Maintain integrity

Matthew 7:24-27

"Therefore everyone who hears these words of mine and puts them into practice is like a wise man who built his house on the rock. The rain came down, the streams rose, and the winds blew and beat against that house; yet it did not fall, because it had its foundation on the rock. But everyone who hears these words of mine and does not put them into practice is like a foolish man who built his house on sand. The rain came down, the streams rose, and the winds blew and beat against that house, and it fell with a great crash."

Congratulations for making it to the second half of the 40 Days. One characteristic of a good learner is integrity: the state of being whole and undivided. There needs to be a healthy wholeness in our spiritual, physical and emotional life. It is built by receiving something in the Scriptures and letting it penetrate everything. The Scriptures speak deeply in order to do their transforming work. Our response is acting upon it. Integrity is the result.

Jesus said, "Everyone then who hears these words of mine and does them will be like a wise man who built his house on the rock." It will stand the test of difficulty because the Scriptures are integrated into life. Taking action on something that Jesus said, exercises our integrity. The Scriptures are like a mirror, when we see something wrong we try to fix it.

As you read the Scriptures this week, ask God to show you where there is any difference between the way you are living and the way He thinks is best.

For Reflection:
- Is integrity something you find easy or difficult?
- What does it mean to build your house on the rock?

Make Life Count:
- Imagine taking an x-ray of the foundations of your life and imagine a flood coming. How do you think you will cope? Ask Jesus to show you how you could have him become a better foundation?

Divine Truth

Meet this week to discuss DIVINE TRUTH 2: Days 15 to 21

Remember that you are building new patterns through your interaction in helping others in their growth. One pattern is that as a leader you could do *ALL* the talking, give *ALL* the answers and expect that the person will remember everything. Another pattern is that you ASK questions and listen and help the person discover what the Lord is saying. The first pattern is fast but there will always be a dependency that you have to be present to give the right answer. The second pattern is much slower but people gain the tools to learn for themselves.

Participate as a fellow learner and not as an expert. If a question comes up, ask what other's think. Be vulnerable yourself in sharing what you are learning. Your example of honesty and integrity helps establish a pattern of being authentic. With a group, don't feel you have to comment on every comment rather bounce the conversation back to the group by asking, "What do other's think?"

Learning **to be with** the other as a friend and fellow traveler is an important value. If the person feels valued, listened to, and cared for, it does not matter whether all of the lessons are discussed. If they are encouraged, they will want to come back next week.

1. Ask what stands out in this week with the focus on **D**ivine Truth, the **D** in the DNA of Discipleship.
2. Be sure your own devotional time is meaningful. It does not have to be in the same passages if you have done this before, but it does need to be authentic.
3. It can be good to simply practice together 7 Minutes with God. Give people a clear model to imitate and do it together if the person Is having difficulty.
4. Next week we will start looking at **N**urturing relationships, the **N** in the DNA of Discipleship

Day 22: Make the transition

2 Peter 3:18

But grow in the grace and knowledge of our Lord and Savior Jesus Christ. To him be glory both now and forever! Amen.

Just as the **DNA** carries the genetic code in our bodies so that cells grow and reproduce, so we can think of steps which help give a blueprint for growth in discipleship. In the **DNA** of discipleship:
The **D** stands for **D**ivine truth from reading the Scriptures. We can daily practice 7 minutes with God, as a way to begin.
The **N** stands for **N**urturing relationships. In community we nurture through asking questions and listening to each other.

- How have you perceived the presence of God this week?
- How have you responded?
- What risks have you taken by faith?
- What are you learning?
- How can we help?

Meet with others to discuss these questions and the daily Scripture readings then help each other take action. Make notes of what stands out to you so you can use it in your discussion. The **A** stands for **A**dvancing the mission which we will look at later.

For Reflection:

- What is the role of **DNA** in our bodies?
- What are spiritual patterns that have helped you grow?

Make Life Count:

- Write down the names of 2 or 3 people you could discuss these questions with. Pray about inviting one of them for a coffee. (If you are in a small group, send them an email to say you are praying for them today. And pray for them!)

Nurturing Relationships

Day 23: Examine yourself

2 Corinthians 13:5

Examine yourselves to see whether you are in the faith; test yourselves. Do you not realize that Christ Jesus is in you—unless, of course, you fail the test?

Check your progress on how you have been going so far. It can be helpful to know how frequently you are engaging the Scriptures. Try varying the time, frequency and Scripture passages and observe what happens. (Remember **D** for **D**ivine truth)

The questions to develop Nurturing relationships are:

- *How have you perceived the presence of God this week?*
- *How have you responded?*
- *What risks have you taken by faith?*
- *What are you learning?*
- *How can we be of help?*

Try using these questions with someone this week.
(Remember **N** for **N**urturing relationships.)
Have you been praying daily for laborers? The alarm on the cellphone reminds you to pause for a few seconds and to ask God for laborers. Have you noticed anything happening because you are praying what Jesus indicated? (Remember **A** for **A**dvancing the mission)
We would love to hear from you what is happening .
(Reply via email: coaching@networkchurch.ca)

For Reflection:

- What does the **DNA**. of discipleship stand for?

- Is this a helpful pattern to use?

Make Life Count:

- Sit in silence for a few minutes and ask Jesus to examine your heart concerning learning from His Scriptures, the relationships that nurture you and your prayer for labourers for the harvest. What do you sense him saying?

Nurturing Relationships

Day 24: Hear the gentle whisper

1 Kings 19:12-13

After the earthquake came a fire, but the Lord was not in the fire. And after the fire came a gentle whisper. When Elijah heard it, he pulled his cloak over his face and went out and stood at the mouth of the cave.
Then a voice said to him, "What are you doing here, Elijah?"

How have you perceived the presence of God this week? The prophet Elijah was very discouraged and he needed to hear from God. The Scriptures said that an earthquake and fire and mighty wind passed by but Elijah could not hear God in those things. Then there was a still, small voice that Elijah heard God speaking to him. God asked him, 'What was he doing there?' And Elijah explained himself and received fresh instructions. Isn't it amazing that God asks us questions to help us think and to help us to be open to new ideas? Sometimes as we read, it is only a whisper, a nudge, a new thought or question. Sometimes it is connecting an earlier thought to a new idea. Sometimes it is by writing something down or explaining your thought to another person that helps you understand what God is saying.

For Reflection:

- Has God spoken to you through wind, earthquake, fire or a small voice?
- What other word would you use to describe how Jesus speaks to you?

Make Life Count:

- Write a short email to one of your *encouragers* and tell him/her someway you have perceived God's presence this week.

Nurturing Relationships

Day 25: Apply your faith

Hebrews 11:6

And without faith it is impossible to please God, because anyone who comes to him must believe that he exists and that he rewards those who earnestly seek him.

Nurturing relationships mean taking risks. We risk when we tell someone we love them. We risk when we become vulnerable. Risk is an action that shows that our faith is real. If I said that I believe that a certain chair could hold me, by faith I could say "yes it is strong enough" but really only by taking the risk of sitting on it, can I show that my faith is genuine. Sometimes we believe certain things by faith, like God's love for us and his forgiveness. This leads to risking loving and forgiving someone else. The more you can take risks of faith, the more you will become aware of God working around you. Like reaching out to help someone with a need, or suggesting something helpful or offering to do something with another person. These risks will deepen our relationships both with God and others.

For Reflection:

- Think of one risk you have taken that really seemed to work well.
- Think of one that didn't. What was the difference?

Make Life Count:

- Take a step of risk today. Do something that could fail, but where you trust God for strength and success.

The DNA of Discipleship

Nurturing Relationships

Day 26: Help carry others' burden

Galatians 6:2

Carry each other's burdens, and in this way you will fulfill the law of Christ.

How do we nurture relationships? We nurture relationships by being with another, listening, or praying regularly for that person. We can follow-up later by asking how the problem is going. God may give us a verse to encourage the other person. It might come from your reading where you can mark it as a favorite to be discussed later. Sometimes we help by hearing the confession of another and we pray and speak over them God's forgiveness. God may show us a way to serve the person, like driving them somewhere, helping them to pay for something, cooking food or helping to clean or fix something. Sometimes we think of a question that helps us understand the problem. We can communicate how much we care and accept the person. These actions make love real and help us to bear each other's burdens which Paul said fulfilled Christ's law.

For Reflection:

- How have you been helped by someone else in the faith?
- What type of things count as a burden that needs help to carry?

Make Life Count:

- Do some concrete step of action to help carry someone else's burden today.

Nurturing Relationships

Day 27: Ask questions

Mark 10:51

"What do you want me to do for you?" Jesus asked him. The blind man said, "Rabbi, I want to see."

If you are doing these 40 days but are having trouble finding meaningful fellowship where you live, then learn to ask more questions. At times we may feel we have no one who cares about us. We may visit a church that feels cold or unfriendly. We may enter and leave and no one greets us. No one seems to care or they are too busy talking to their friends. We may find a small group but it takes time to feel at home.

One thing we can do is ask people more questions. Listen to their story. Find out how they are unique. Look for common experiences. Be open to learn about anything you can from their lives.

Asking good questions is an art that comes by practice. If we persevere we will find others who want to grow and we can encourage each other. Sometimes the right question is more important than the right answer.

For Reflection:

- Why did Jesus ask the man what he wanted?
- How would you answer Jesus' question?

Make Life Count:

- Go for a walk and answer the question that Jesus asks "What do you want me to do for you?"

The DNA of Discipleship

Nurturing Relationships

Day 28: Let the Spirit teach you

John 14:26

But the Advocate, the Holy Spirit, whom the Father will send in my name, will teach you all things and will remind you of everything I have said to you.

The Holy Spirit is our teacher. This is good news because he is always with us, he comes along side and he teaches us everything we need. When Jesus left he sent the Holy Spirit to take his place and he is universally present with his people. Jesus said that this was better than if he himself stayed. This means that our interaction with God is not just historical but it is continuous, in every moment and at all times. This is spectacular in scope and points to an ongoing intimacy and guidance that is personal and transformative. The Holy Spirit is everything we need, just in time, and in the right amount. We never need feel alone or forgotten. Our situation is always before his sight. He is already working around us and invites us to join in. Now that is learning from God.

For Reflection:

- Do you feel that the Holy Spirit is teaching you?
- What would you like to learn from the Holy Spirit?

Make Life Count:

- Ask God to remind you of anything you need to remember throughout the day. At day's end, review what happened.

Nurturing Relationships

Meet this week to discuss NURTURING RELATIONSHIPS: Days 22 to 28

These two weeks of the 40 Days of Discipleship focusses on *Nurturing relationships* through learning to ask questions in community. Jesus said to build our house on the rock so that *WHEN* the flood comes we will be able to resist and stand firm. He didn't say '*IF*' the flood comes, but '*WHEN*' it comes. There is a term to describe people who do not learn to build on the rock of Christ before flood time: they are called VICTIMS.

Maturing in Christ is no small thing. The people you encourage are looking to you for a living example of how to grow. You are Christ's hands, feet, mouth and ears.' Being with' this person is more than studying passages. It is listening, learning together, laughing, crying, relaxing, dreaming, praying and serving. It is a journey together. It is practicing the one-another's of loving, forgiving, supporting and the dozens of other ways this can be practiced.

The questions we can ask to nurture relationships require a context of trust. We need to earn the right to ask these by demonstrating our commitment to the person and not just an activity. We need to be trustworthy not to gossip what we hear.

We also need to be free to adapt the questions to our context. The principal is what do we see God doing, and hear God speaking and do we respond. How can we help each other to do that?

1.   Start with asking people what stood out from the readings this week.
2.   Include the questions to nurture relationships as they are listed in the lesson (Day 22).
    a. How have you perceived the presence of God this week?
    b. How have you responded?
    c. What risks have you taken by faith?
    d. What are you learning?
    e. How can we help?
3. Do not be so focused in following the plan that you can't listen to what God is saying through each other.

4. Reflect on the meeting afterward as you pray for the participants. What do you feel went well or was someone struggling? Talk with God about this.

Day 29: Trust the Spirit's intercession

Romans 8:26

In the same way, the Spirit helps us in our weakness. We do not know what we ought to pray for, but the Spirit himself intercedes for us through wordless groans.

Have you found it difficult putting your prayer into words? The Scriptures say we do not know how to pray as we should but that the Spirit asks for us with groans too deep for words. The Scriptures also say we have a great high priest, Jesus, who lives to make intercession for us. This is a real comfort. Your prayer or mine would get nowhere if it were not for the Holy Spirit and Christ's help. We don't have to fuss about saying things exactly right. We can be like young children talking to our parents. They understand what we mean. God changes our words into acceptable prayers.

Stop for a moment before you pray to become aware that your words are nothing without Christ, yet through Him we can come boldly into his presence. Become aware that He has done everything necessary by his death, resurrection and going to heaven, to make our prayers reach God. Thank God for such a Savior. Tomorrow we will learn how to practice this conversationally.

For Reflection:

- When have you felt that God heard your prayer?
- Is this the same as God answering your prayer?

Make Life Count:

- Today spend your prayer time in silence remembering that the Holy Spirit is interceding for you.

Nurturing Relationships

Day 30: Pray conversationally

Hebrews 4:14

Therefore, since we have a great high priest who has ascended into heaven, Jesus the Son of God, let us hold firmly to the faith we profess.

Conversational prayer is like any conversation. Someone speaks and someone listens and then responds based on the topic. One person doesn't talk all the time. People don't have to repeat themselves in order to be listened to. The conversation flows between all participants.

One way to practice conversational prayer as a group is to decide to say very short prayers where we listen in between. This avoids having to make the prayer 'sound right'. In order to practice, make the prayers VERY short, like how much can you say comfortably, without taking a breath. Then pause and let someone else continue. Don't be afraid of silence. You can take a breath and continue when there is another pause. You will find that it is easier to keep involved, to pay attention and to sense God guiding your prayer time. There are many different ways to pray, so use the invitation, "Let's pray conversationally" as a way to help new comers feel comfortable speaking their words out loud.

For Reflection:

- Do you feel comfortable praying out loud?
- What does God think about your prayer?

Make Life Count:

- Try conversational prayer with another person. Be particularly mindful of keeping what you say very short, so you can listen to what others say. Be comfortable with silence.

The DNA of Discipleship

Nurturing Relationships

Day 31: Pray in Jesus' name

John 14:13-14

And I will do whatever you ask in my name, so that the Father may be glorified in the Son. You may ask me for anything in my name, and I will do it.

Why do we say 'In Jesus name' when we finish a prayer? Does any prayer suddenly becomes acceptable because we add 'in Jesus name" at the end?

Saying 'In Jesus name' when we pray is a reminder that we are asking what we think Jesus wants and deserves in that situation. We are asking according to his worthiness and victory on the cross. He died to make such a prayer answerable. So we think about that when we ask. In some countries children go to a corner store and make purchases on their parents' account. If they ask for a quart of milk or a loaf of bread they get it. If they ask for 5 kilos of candy they don't. By asking in their parents' name, the store owner gives then what their parents would want.

When we read the Bible, we find out what God wants, and this guides us to ask in Jesus' name.

For Reflection:

- Have you ever wondered why we put 'In Jesus' name at the end of the prayer?
- What is the value of repeating this phrase in your prayer?

Make Life Count:

- Instead of saying "In Jesus' name" at the end of the prayer, for every phrase ask yourself "Is this what Jesus wants?"

The DNA of Discipleship

Nurturing Relationships

Day 32: Receive his love

Ephesians 3:14-19

For this reason I kneel before the Father, from whom every family in heaven and on earth derives its name. I pray that out of his glorious riches he may strengthen you with power through his Spirit in your inner being, so that Christ may dwell in your hearts through faith. And I pray that you, being rooted and established in love, may have power, together with all the Lord's holy people, to grasp how wide and long and high and deep is the love of Christ, and to know this love that surpasses knowledge—that you may be filled to the measure of all the fullness of God.

God the Father surrounds us with love. Discipleship is not about earning God's favor or adding something to improve the Gospel. The oldest, most mature, Jesus' learner still needs the shed blood of Christ as much as the new born in Christ. The love of God the Father is perfectly shown through Jesus and his life and death, so we cannot be more loved because we are good disciples. He loves us through his Son, perfectly, eternally and unconditionally. He is the father of the prodigal, always yearning for our best, longing for our restoration when we stray and celebrating the victory when we return. We interact with Father, Son and Holy Spirit in community, the Holy Trinity, seeking our growth and transformation, and doing everything necessary to make it happen. This helps keep our personal efforts in perspective.

For Reflection:

- What else can God do to help you grow?
- When do you feel most loved by God?

Make Life Count:

- Find a private place to kneel down and pray today's Scripture out loud.

Nurturing Relationships

Day 33: Pray 'Our Father...'

Matthew 6:9-13

This, then, is how you should pray:
"'Our Father in heaven, hallowed be your name, your
kingdom come, your will be done, on earth as it is in heaven.
Give us today our daily bread.
And forgive us our debts, as we also have forgiven our debtors.
And lead us not into temptation, but deliver us from the evil
one."

We learn to pray by praying. When the disciples saw how Jesus prayed they asked him to teach them. Instead of giving a complicate theology, he taught them a simple prayer that starts 'Our Father in heaven'. It is brief (about 50 words) and covers praise and petition, both for the very practical (our daily bread) and for the theological (the coming kingdom and the holy name of God). This pattern is used by millions of Christians from every background and tradition.

The important thing is that this prayer is to be used. We learn as we pray together. It is not for theological debate but for talking with our Father in heaven. I like to imagine when praying this how a child talks while nestled in a parent's lap with such intimacy and trust. The phrases can pattern your prayer for broader development or they can be prayed as is. We learn to pray by praying.

For Reflection:

* Did you grow up with this prayer?
* Do you find it helpful?

Make Life Count:

* Pray the Lord's Prayer out loud. Find a private place and kneel down while you pray it.

Nurturing Relationships

Day 34: Be transparent

Matthew 5:16

In the same way, let your light shine before others, that they may see your good deeds and glorify your Father in heaven.

Transparency is another characteristic of a Jesus' learner. The way we truly are, is never hidden from God. His Scriptures can cut to the bone showing us what we are like. When we are transparent, others can see what is going on and encourage us. It means we don't have to pretend to be something we are not. We can be real about our struggles and our hopes. We can accept people for whom they really are and accept ourselves, since God has accepted us in Jesus.
Transparency is necessary if we really want to encourage one another to love and good works. We let His light shine into our lives and receive motivation and direction. We don't have to be like Adam and Eve who hid from God after they sinned. We maintain healthy boundaries but are open to learn. We reflect on who we are in Christ in the openness and safety of our faith community. Shine your Light in and through us for Your glory, O Lord.

For Reflection:

- Do you think Jesus was a transparent person?
- How is he an example for us?

Make Life Count:

- On a scale of 1 to 10, how transparent a person are you? Is that what you want?

Nurturing Relationships

Day 35: Be vulnerable

Luke 22:42

"Father, if you are willing, take this cup from me; yet not my will, but yours be done."

Vulnerability is a third characteristic of a learner. It means we are open to change. We could get hurt. At appropriate times, we share our struggles, our feelings and our hopes. Because we are vulnerable, we need to learn to be gentle with one another and respectful of the trust people have in us. We need to be careful how we talk about each other and not gossip. There are many commands in the New Testament that mention doing things one to another: Love, forgive, support, not judge, serve, submit and exhort. These are practiced with others and impossible to do by ourselves. It is not someone else's job. It is not a program. It is not once-a-week.

Integrity, transparency and vulnerability are three marks of a growing Jesus' learner and are evidence of a life being transformed by Him. These characteristics should describe us and should affect everything.

For Reflection:

- Where do you see Jesus being vulnerable?
- What are the costs and benefits of being vulnerable?

Make Life Count:

- Thirteen days ago you made a list of 2 or 3 people (your 'encouragers') that you hope to connect with spiritually. Have you managed to meet anyone yet? If not, write an email now and invite them to connect.

The DNA of Discipleship

Advancing the Mission

Meet this week to discuss NURTURING RELATIONSHIPS 2: Days 29 to 35

This week many of the readings relate to the nurturing relationship of prayer. Help people to pray conversationally by saying a simple phrase or idea; what you can say with one breath. Then someone else continues the conversation (Day 30). Think of a normal conversation with talking and listening. People don't repeat what is already said, but they add to the conversation a thought that flows in the same theme.

This skill is more than just giving everyone an opportunity to pray. There is an interdependence of listening to the Spirit together where the conversation is supernaturally guided. It is also a comfort that the Holy Spirit intercedes for us, so that we do not have to be concerned about the exact wording in forming our prayer. Brevity in prayer also helps others pay attention and keep their minds from wandering. As always, the leader's example is important.

How do you feel people are doing? Are they encouraged? Are you praying for them? Is the saltiness of Jesus making them thirsty for more? How may your nurturing relationship deepen with others in your faith community?

Use these discussion questions or adapt them as needed:

- How have you perceived the presence of God this week?
- How have you responded?
- What risks have you taken by faith?
- What are you learning?
- How can we help?

Day 36: Obey the Divine Mandate

Luke 10:2

He told them, "The harvest is plentiful, but the workers are few.
Ask the Lord of the harvest, therefore, to send out workers into
his harvest field.

In our Spiritual D.N.A: the **D** stands for **D**ivine truth and we engage with the Scriptures. The **N** stands for **N**urturing relationships and we ask each other questions.

The **A** stands for **A**dvancing the mission. The Apostles were ones sent by God. We join in God's mission by praying for laborers for the harvest. In Luke 10:2 Jesus said, "The harvest is plentiful but the workers are few. Ask the Lord of the harvest to send out workers into his harvest." It is a strange command but Jesus said we should pray this way.

A tool to remember to pray is to set your cell phone alarm to 2 minutes after 10 am or pm where 10:02 reminds us of the Luke 10:2 passage and the need to pray. Do not under-estimate this simple prayer as God will begin to do show you amazing things you can do as you pray for more laborers.

For Reflection:

- When have you ever felt you are on a mission?
- Where do you see needs where God might be sending you to help?

Make Life Count:

- Set the alarm on your phone to 10:02 and take 1 minute each day at that time to pray for workers to be sent to the harvest. Try this and see what happens.

Advancing the Mission

Day 37: Answer the call

Isaiah 6:8

Then I heard the voice of the Lord saying, "Whom shall I send? And who will go for us?"

Harvesting crops is good because it feeds people. This type of work can be hot and tiring but it has a great reward. When we pray for harvest workers, Jesus said to ask God to cast or thrust them into the harvest. This is the same verb used to cast out demons. It is violent and messy. It is abrupt and sudden. We don't ease into it. We are fired into the harvest. We don't wade in the shallow end. We jump off the deep end. This is something we can't necessarily control or manage. It happens to us. So keep your eyes open. You may find that you are fired into a whole new situation where you stop being a consumer of religious truth and start to desperately hang on to God, way out of your comfort zone. This is a risky prayer but as we pray for harvest workers, the Lord invites us to say like Isaiah, "Here am I , send me!"

For Reflection:

- Why did Jesus use an agricultural expression for something so important?
- What term would Isaiah have used?

Make Life Count:

- Go for a walk to somewhere you can see a skyline or people or traffic. Imagine God asking you 'Who will go for us'. Tell Him your response.

Advancing the Mission

Day 38: Give freely

Matthew 10:8

Heal the sick, raise the dead, cleanse those who have leprosy, drive out demons. Freely you have received; freely give.

Do you want be a better learner...to pay more attention to what God is saying and doing? Do you want to increase the risk factor? Are you hungry for more? What ideas do you have about next steps? Where can you respond with more heart and soul? What would it look like if God did precisely what you have been asking for?

Consider taking the second series of the 40 Days of discipleship on the 5 verbs of learning. It will still be just a minute a day, but you will be encouraged to help someone else along the path by showing them how to start the 40 days with God as you continue in the next series. You will learn how to deepen the D.N.A. pattern for yourself, and for your friend and are encouraged to meet weekly to discuss the questions that build nurturing relationship. You will discover how God wants to reveal His kingdom through you in surprising new ways. When these forty days are finished, select the next series to continue.

For Reflection:

- What has happened in your life over the 40 days?
- Is this what you imagined?

Make Life Count:

- List how you have observed changes in your relationship with God through these 40 days. Tell somebody.

The DNA of Discipleship

Advancing the Mission

Day 39: Keep growing

Jude 1:20-21

But you, dear friends, by building yourselves up in your most holy faith and praying in the Holy Spirit, keep yourselves in God's love as you wait for the mercy of our Lord Jesus Christ to bring you to eternal life.

We have looked at the **DNA** of discipleship (**D**ivine truth, **N**urturing relationships and **A**dvancing the mission) and practiced the being, doing and thinking related to faith in Jesus. We said at the beginning that 40 days was a time of testing where something significant was going to happen. Do you have any idea what that might be? Don't worry if it is not yet clear because sometimes growth is invisible. Sometimes it is something that others can see but we don't see in ourselves. Sometimes it is a feeling or a conviction but sometimes it is simply having survived the test. Rejoice! Thank God! Celebrate the accomplishment! Telling someone else as your example of perseverance may be of great encouragement and an example to follow. And express your gratitude to God for such a Savior as Jesus Christ.

For Reflection:
- Are you interested in continuing with the next 40 days of discipleship?
  (https://www.getdrip.com/forms/2986484/submissions/new **You must respond to a confirmation email to continue to Series 2)**)
- Do you have someone to invite to this DNA Series while you go on to the next one? This could be the best step of learning you make in this series.

Make Life Count:
- **Write an email inviting someone** to take Series 1 while you begin Series 2. Both Series are designed to work together, so as you continue in the second series you can encourage someone in the first one.
- **Copy/paste this sample invitation into an email:** *I have just finished a very helpful series I receive by daily email on how to be a better follower of Jesus. I would like to invite you to sign up at this link:* https://www.getdrip.com/forms/45989233/submissions/new *Confirm your subscription from your email inbox.*

Advancing the Mission

Day 40: Join the Million Laborer Challenge

1 Thessalonians 5:11

Therefore encourage one another and build each other up, just as in fact you are doing.

Congratulations for finishing these 40 days. Here is the Million Laborer Challenge for you to consider. We want to help 1 million Jesus' followers in the next 4 years so they can serve God as volunteers. They may do something as simple as helping someone engage the Scriptures. They can encourage someone to grow, and support them in prayer. They can discuss the nurturing relationship questions and share highlights from the Scripture readings throughout the week. They are not experts, just fellow learners. If asked a difficult question they can say, "I don't know but I can try to find out". Their own life is an example and a pattern that the others can imitate.

This can be the start of a lifetime of encouraging others. If you don't know anyone to start with, then keep praying Luke 10:2 for more workers. God will show you who you could invite and together deepen your spiritual journey with Jesus. Series 2 is part of the Million Laborer Challenge. We hope to see you there.

For Reflection:

- Do you want to be part of a million workers encouraging others?
- Who can you invite to join you?

Make Life Count:

- Write a comment to encourage others in the 40 days of Discipleship and post it at our page in Facebook https://www.facebook.com/40daysofdiscipleship/

  Don't underestimate the profound impact this could have.

Advancing the Mission

Meet this Week to discuss ADVANCING THE MISSION: Day 36 to 40

This week is one of celebration and of challenge in finishing this series of 40 days. Celebrate every step of progress in understanding the DNA of discipleship. If someone looked at only one lesson there is still something to celebrate. Giving people opportunity to express gratitude to God for the experience is an important celebration. Helping them summarize what they have learned is another tool for celebration.

What progress do you observe? Where would you like to see more growth? What has been your personal experience of growth as a leader? What do you need? Please feel free to share that with us.

This week is also one of challenge. From the very start we want to introduce the idea of praying for labourers which moves us out of a self-centered focus. Be sure people understand that this prayer is very simple and provides more opportunities for people to get the help they need. More labourers means more people will have an opportunity to celebrate their growth like you are celebrating now.

We also need to ask people what they would like to do next. Some may feel they have enough for the time being and others may want more. No one needs to feel pressured to continue. Those who choose to continue and wish to receive the 40 days via email, will need to confirm the invitation sent to their inbox.

The second series of 40 Days is about the 5 Verbs of Learning. In this series we will *learn how to learn* by thinking in action verbs and not just in information. You can start at any time and we will periodically send out invitations for people to continue.

We also appreciate your feedback on improvements, suggestions for other topics or resources you would like to share with us.

Finally you may wish to help cover the costs of a person taking the 40 days of discipleship. A gift of $10 will help 10 people participate

www.ingramcontent.com/pod-product-compliance
Lightning Source LLC
Chambersburg PA
CBHW070535030426
42337CB00016B/2216

in this training. You can access a secure site to donate here: http://www.networkchurch.ca/donate/

Use these discussion questions or adapt them as needed:

- How have you perceived the presence of God this week?
- How have you responded?
- What risks have you taken by faith?
- What are you learning?
- How can we help?